IDK

Let's Find Out

How Small Questions Spark Big Changes

Sudeep Mehta

For permissions, please contact:

sudeepnh1@gmail.com

(+91) 9920292240

Published by: Worldwide Photoworks Pvt. Ltd.

Cover design: Purva Mahesh Randive

ISBN: 978-81-991923-2-4

Printed in Mumbai, India by Bhoomi Enterprises

First Edition: 2025

CONTENTS

Acknowledgement

This book was never a solo journey. It grew out of the questions, the sparks, the accidents, and the people who nudged me along the way.

Mana, you remain the unsaid sentence in all that I write.

To Greg and Leonie Marinovich, thank you for giving me the gift of deeper perspective, and for reminding me of a forgotten superpower: the boundless curiosity of a two-year-old. You taught me that wonder is not lost, only misplaced, and you helped me find mine again.

To Ben Böhmer and Monolink, your music has been my creative oxygen. Those soundscapes became portals into imagination, helping me drift into questions I didn't know I needed to ask.

To my friends, the curious creatures, thank you for being my co-conspirators in the pursuit of "what if?"

To my students, you leave me as curious as I hope I leave you. Each question you ask (and sometimes don't ask) pushes me further than I expect. You've made classrooms my most surprising laboratories.

To boredom, my unlikely muse. Artists are restless beings, and in the space between restlessness and boredom, I've stumbled into the ideas that won not just awards, but people. This book is proof that even the dull moments have stories hiding in them.

And finally, to every reader who paused long enough to pick up this book, thank you. Your curiosity keeps mine alive.

Love

Sudeep

Preface

Hey!

If you're reading this, chances are you've either misplaced your curiosity somewhere between deadlines and doomscrolling, or maybe you've never really paused to wonder if curiosity even matters.

Spoiler: It does.

That's the heart of this book. *IDK, Let's Find Out* is about reclaiming the spark we've all lost; the thrill of noticing, questioning, and chasing the things that make us go, "Wait, what?" It's not about colleting answers. It's about learning to sit with "I don't know" and turning it into "let's find out."

Here's the thing: the world right now is built to smother curiosity. Algorithms feed you what you already like. Your brain scrolls past billions of moments a day but rarely stops to chew on them. You're busy; but not awake.

This book is my little rebellion against that.

It's not a lecture. It's a conversation. Part storytelling, part mirror holding, part gentle shove back into the playground of your own brain.

By the end, you won't just agree that curiosity is important. You'll feel it. You'll spot it everywhere. You'll chase it.

Ready?

IDK where this will take you. But let's find out.

Chapter 1

The Autopilot Problem

(a.k.a. How You Become a Background character in Your Own Life)

Let me tell you a secret your brain doesn't want you to know:

You're probably living on default settings.

And default settings are fine for your microwave.

Not for you.

Scene 1: The Walk That Could've Been a Movie

It's a Monday morning. You're walking to class.

Your phone is in your hand, thumbs doing their little up-down TikTok dance. Your brain's tuned into your playlist, somewhere between an Ariana Grande hook and a random podcast clip about why otters hold hands.

You pass a chai stall. Steam rises like tiny white ghosts. A stray dog is curled under the bench, paw twitching mid-dream. A man in a red turban laughs so loudly you can hear it though your AirPods.

But you see none of this.

Why? Because you're running on autopilot mode. The brain's 'energy saver' setting. Your eyes technically see, but your mind's somewhere else entirely.

The tragedy? You just walked past a perfect short film scene… and didn't even know it.

Scene 2: The Carnival That Didn't Matter

True story:

One of my students, let's call her Mahi, once came to class late. I asked why. She mumbled, "Traffic". Fair enough. But later, I overheard her telling a friend she had seen a huge, abandoned carnival on the roadside- rusting rides, faded and torn banners, popcorn machines half-buried in dust.

When I asked, "Why didn't you take a photo? Or at least look around?" she shrugged.

"It was just there."

Just there.

That sentence haunts me.

Because here's the thing: if your brain sees an abandoned carnival and calls it "just there", it's not that the world got boring… it's that *you stopped looking*.

We're All Guilty

Don't get me wrong…I've been Mahi too.

I once travelled to Varanasi for a shoot. Early morning, I crossed the ghats, eyes glues to my phone's GPS, trying to find the 'perfect' sunrise spot. When I finally looked up, I realised I had walked past a sadhu with a monkey on his shoulder, a boy selling paper boats, and a woman painting her boat bright blue.

I'd been in one of the most cinematic places on Earth… and I was basically scrolling my way thought it.

Why Autopilot Exists

Your brain loves shortcuts. It hates wasting energy on stuff it thinks it already knows. So, it turns real life into a predictable slideshow: chai stall, traffic light, shop sign, repeat. This keeps you from going insane in a crowded city, but it also keeps you from *seeing*.

Neuroscientists call it "inattentional blindness". Basically, if you're focused on one thing (like your phone or your own thoughts), your brain will happily ignore everything else, even if it's a man in a gorilla suit walking through a basketball game.

(Yes, that's a real experiment. Look up "Invisible Gorilla Test" later. Mind. Blown.)

The Price you Pay

When you live on autopilot long enough, two things happen:

1. You stop noticing breadcrumbs. Those little "Ooh, what's that?" moments.
2. Your brain stops leaving them for you altogether.

And here's the killer twist: curiosity isn't just about making art or writing stories. It's about staying alive inside. Autopilot turns you into an NPC in your own life.

The Creators Who Never Switched It Off

Some of the most creative people I know have one thing in common: they *notice*.

- Haruki Murakami once wrote an entire short story based on overhearing a single strange sentence in a café.
- Steve Jobs famously got obsessed with calligraphy after wandering into a random college class and that obsession shaped the design of the first Macintosh.

- Vivian Maier, the street photographer, captured magic because she saw what everyone else ignored: a child peeking through a shop window, a man's hat caught in the wind, a face half-hidden in shadow.

These moments where invisible to people in autopilot. But to them, they were gold.

Try This Today:

Your anti-autopilot workout:

- Pocket the phone for the first 10 minutes of your commute.
- Look for three things you've never noticed before. The stranger the better.
- Bonus points: Take one photo. No filters. Just… notice.

Autopilot is great for long flight. Not for living.

You didn't sign up to be a background character. You're the main character. Act like it.

Chapter 2

The Two-Year-Old Superpower

(a.k.a. How You Once Knew the Secret to the Universe and Forgot It)

Let's time-travel for a moment.

You're two years old. Your entire life is a walking, babbling investigation.

You point at a bird. "Why?"

You point at the sky. "Why?"

You point at the fan. "Why?"

Your parents answer for a while, but after 47th "WHY?", they give up and say something like, "Because God made it that way", which is adult-speak for "I'm out of explanations, kid."

You Were Born Curious

That relentless "why" phase wasn't just you being annoying; it was you downloading the world. Your brain at that age was running the ultimate curiosity software.

Neuroscience backs this up; toddlers ask an average for 100+ questions a day. That's not a random number; that's a survival tool. Questions build mental maps, connect patterns, and help you figure out how the world works.

And then… school happened.

How We Lost It

School teaches us answers, not questions. By the time we hit our teens, we've learned that asking too many questions:

- Makes you 'look dumb'.
- Slows the class down.
- Gets you that side-eye from the teacher.

So we stop.

We stop even when the question is burning in our heads. We stop because we think everyone already knows. We stop because silence feels safer.

True Story: The Question That Changed Everything

Back in 1995, a guy names James Dyson (yes, the vacuum guy) asked a question no one else in is field bothered to ask: "Why do vacuum cleaners lose suction over time?"

Everyone else accepted it as "just how vacuums are". Dyson didn't. He spent **5 years** and **5,127 prototypes** chasing the answer. Today, he's worth over $20 billion. All because he didn't retire his inner toddler.

Closer to Home

One of my photography students once asked in class, "Why do shadows sometimes look blue in photos?"

Half the room rolled their eyes. But that one question led her down a rabbit hole into colour temperature, the physics of light, and eventually, no joke, her winning an award for a photo series on urban nightscapes.

That's the magic. One 'silly' question can launch an entire creative universe.

Pop Culture Proof

- Pixar's movie WALL-E started with the question: "What if the last robot on Earth was just... lonely?"

- The Harry Potter series was born because J.K. Rowling asked herself: "What if a kid found out he was a wizard… but didn't know it until 11?"
- Even Elon Musk, love him or hate him, started SpaceX with: "Why hasn't anyone made space travel cheaper yet?"

Questions are the seeds. Everything else grows from them.

Relearning the Superpower

You don't have to start every sentence with "Why" like a toddler (although, try it for a day- it's fun). But you can train yourself to:

- Question the obvious:
  "Why do we cut cake this way?"
- Challenge the rules
  "What if we did it backwards?"
- Ask what's missing
  "What am I not seeing here?"

Mini Challenge:

Pick one ordinary thing in your day- a spoon, a building, your bus route; and ask five questions about it.

Even if the first three feel dumb, keep going.

By question five, you'll be somewhere unexpected.

Why This Matters

The moment you stop asking questions, your brain goes back to autopilot (hello, Chapter 1). But the moment you start again, the world cracks open. Suddenly there's more texture, more possibilities, more life.

So yeah, your toddler self wasn't annoying. They were a genius.

Chapter 3

Learning to Notice the Weird Studd

(a.k.a. Why the Best Stories Hide in the Corners of Your Vision)

Here's a fun trust about the world:

It is absolutely, wildly, bizarrely full of weirdness.

You just stopped noticing.

Not because the weird stuff disappeared; but because your brain, in its 'helplessness', filters it out. It assumes you don't need it to survive.

The problem?

That 'weird' is exactly where the good ideas live.

True Story: The Red Balloon

Vivian Maier, the now-famous street photographer, once captured an image of a single red balloon tangled in the branches of a tree. That was it. No people. No city skyline. Just a balloon.

But the photo feels like a story, because she noticed. Hundreds of others must've walked past it, thinking "meh, balloon". But she saw the contrast of red against grey, the way it clung to the branches like a stubborn dream.

Weird Is Fuel for Creation

Some of the most creative works come from noticing something off:

- Newton saw an apple fall and asked, "Why down? Why not sideways?"
- Salvador Dali saw melting cheese and turned it into *The Persistence of Memory*.
- Hayao Miyazaki (*Spirited Away*) noticed a young girl looking bored at her parents' dinner party- and thought: "What if there's a magical world just waiting for kids like her?"

Weird isn't noise. It's the doorway.

How to Spot It

You can train your brain to notice the odd, the unusual, the stuff that 'doesn't fit'. Try this:

1. Mismatch Hunt: Look for something that doesn't belong- a palm tree in the middle of a concrete lot, a man in a business suit riding a kids' bicycle.
2. Colour Spy: Choose a colour in the morning. Spend your day noticing where it pops up in unexpected places.
3. Out-of-Place Sound: Listen for something that doesn't match the environment- a temple bell in a busy street, or laughter in a library.

Closer to Home

A student of mine once did this exercise and came back with a story about a lone pink shoe lying on the roadside. Instead of just shrugging it off, she started imagining who it belonged to. Lost in a breakup? Dropped while running for a bus?

It wasn't the shoe that was special. It was her attention.

Mini Challenge:

Tomorrow, give yourself a **Weird Quota**:

- Find 3 things that make you go "Huh?"
- Write them down or photograph them.

- Ask yourself, "What story could explain this?"

Do it for a week, and you'll have more story seeds than you know what to do with.

Chapter 4

Asking Better Questions

(a.k.a. The Upgrade from "What is this?" to

"What could this be?")

Here's something most people don't realise:

The quality of your curiosity depends on the quality of your questions.

Bad questions get you boring answers.

Good questions crack open wormholes to other universes.

The 'Okay' Questions vs. The 'Ooh' Question

Imagine you see a crumpled flyer on the ground.

- Okay Question: "What's this?" → Answer: "A flyer." End of story.
- Ooh Question: "Who made this? Why was it thrown away? Did it fail? Or was it part of something bigger?"

That second type of question makes your brain put on a detective hat. Suddenly, you're not just identifying. You're imagining.

True Story: The Blue Door in Jodhpur

A few years ago, I was wandering the blue city of Jodhpur. Most tourists were taking the usual Instagram shots of the painted walls. But I noticed one particular door: deep indigo, with a cracked brass handle and scratch marks around the keyhole.

The average question would've been: "Why is it blue?"

But I asked: "Who scratches a door that much? What's the story?"

Later, over chai, an old man told me the scratches were from goats; a family used to keep them indoors at night, and they'd paw at the door to be let out in the morning.

If I hadn't asked the specific question, I'd have missed the image of goats waking up to the sunrise in a little blue house.

Why 'Why' is just the Start

'Why' is a powerful word; but it's just Level 1.

Great questioners mix it up with:

- **What if…?** (What if the moon was actually hollow?)
- **How come…**? (How come trains still run late in 2025?)
- **Who else**…? (Who else would care about this abandoned factory?)
- **What would happen if…?** (What would happen if we removed all traffic lights in the city?)

These aren't just information-seeking questions; they're imagination-stretching questions.

Pop Culture Examples

- Pixar's *Inside Out* came from: "What if emotions were actual characters?"
- Nike's Air Jordan campaign started with: "What would happen if a basketball shoe had its own myth?"
- Banksy's street art often makes people ask: "Who is this person?" – and that question fuels his entire mystique.

The Coffee Shop Test

Here's an exercise I use with my students:

Go to a café. Pick a random person. Ask yourself 5 increasingly strange, specific questions about them (all in your head, of course; don't be creepy).

Example:

1. What are they drinking?
2. Did they choose it because it's their favourite or because it was on discount?
3. Who taught them to hold a cup like that?
4. What was their morning like before that came here?
5. If they had to disappear and start a new life today, where would they go?

By question 5, your brain is already spinning stories. That's the point.

Closer to Home

One random day, I was staring at a surveillance monitor showing tiny boxes: each a live feed from various CCTV cameras. And then, boom! My brain went, *what if* I could watch multiple screens at once and a story starts unfolding across them? That tiny spark turned into a silent short crime/thriller film for my Harvard filmmaking assignment. It not only got me full marks but later bagged 23 international awards, represented India at Dubai Expo

2020, and even screened twice at a Hollywood studio. Not because the story was great, because this style of storytelling was something that the global audience experienced for the very first time. All because of one question: *what if?* That's the real magic- curiosity flips your perspective, turns the mundane into cinematic gold, and sometimes, gets you places you didn't even dare to dream of. So, next time your brain throws a "what if" at you, don't scroll past it- run with it.

One of my friends, Rishi, used this technique on 2 similar looking umbrellas with one small unnoticeable distinction. His question: "What would happen if these 2 umbrellas could tell their stories?" The answer turned into a short film I later made for my assignment at Harvard. It went viral.

All because of one better question.

Mini Challenge:

Pick an everyday object right now- your shoes, your pen, the glass on your desk- and write down **five questions** about it.

By the fifth, make it so specific or weird that you start laughing. That's when you're getting somewhere.

Chapter 5

How to Chase a Rabbit Hole

(a.k.a. Why Wasting Time Can Sometimes Be the Smartest Thing You Do)

Here's a confession:

Some of my best ideas came from 'wasting time'.

And by wasting time, I mean falling down rabbit holes.

You know that moment you click one video about "how to make sourdough" and somehow end up three hours later watching a documentary on medieval bread-making techniques in rural France.

Why Rabbit Holes Matter

A rabbit hole is when your curiosity drags you somewhere unexpected, unrelated, and oddly specific- and instead of resisting, you follow it.

Most people fight this. They think it's 'distracting'. But for a creative mind, these tangents are gold mines. Because:

- They connect unrelated ideas.
- They lead to niche knowledge no one else has.
- They make your brain *play*.

True Story: The Penguin That Made a Movie

I once read a random fact that some penguins 'propose' by giving each other pebbles. That was it- one weird sentence in an article.

But I couldn't stop thinking about it. Why pebbles? Do they look for the prettiest one? Do penguins reject pebbles?

Hours of research later, I'd learned about penguin courtship rituals, colony politics, and even a real-life case where a male penguin stole pebbles from others. That single curiosity detour inspired a short animated film script about a 'criminal' penguin running a pebble-smuggling racket.

It never would've happened if I'd told myself, *"Eh, that's irrelevant. Back to work."*

The YouTube Spiral Theory

There's an old saying: "the most interesting ideas live two links away from where you started"

Example:

- Start: Watching a tutorial on portrait lighting.
- Link 1: Video on historical painting and how old masters used light.
- Link 2: Documentary on Rembrandt's 'lost' techniques.

Now you're not just better at lighting; you've also absorbed 17th century artistic philosophy… all because you followed the thread.

Real-World Legends of Rabbit-Holing

- **James Cameron** started researching deep-sea submersibles for Titanic. The rabbit hole led him to actually design one and dive into the Mariana Trench years later.
- **Mary Shelly** was stuck indoors during a bad summer in 1816. She started reading about science experiments with electricity on frogs. Rabbit hole→ *Frankenstein.*
- **Questlove** (The Roots) once said his music collection exists because he kept chasing "one song that reminded me of another song." Until he became an encyclopaedia of grooves.

How to Chase Without Getting Lost

Rabbit holes work best when:

1. You start with a spark- something odd or delightful.
2. You follow the tangents deliberately- not just endless scrolling, but with the intent to learn.
3. You keep souvenirs- notes, screenshots, or photos so you can find your way back.

Think of it like treasure-hunting, not doomscrolling.

Closer to Home

A student of mine once got obsessed with the history of typewriters after watching a single Instagram reel about vintage tech. He ended up buying an old Remington, learning how it worked, and making a photo series on “letters that were never sent.” That project later became part of his design portfolio- and it all started from a random late night curiosity spiral.

Mini Challenge:

Today, allow yourself **one intentional rabbit hole**.

- Pick something you notice or hear about.
- Follow it for at least 30 minutes.
- Write down five unexpected things you discover along the way.

You might not need it now. But trust me- these stored treasures will pay off later when you least expect it.

Chapter 6

Kill the Fear of Looking Dumb

(a.k.a. The Biggest Curiosity Killer of Them All)

Let's be honest.

We've all been there- that moment in class, a meeting, or even a group chat where you have a burning question, but you don't ask it.

Why? Because somewhere ion your head, a little voice whispers:

"What if they think I'm stupid?"

That voice is a liar. And it's costing you more that you think.

The Classroom Freeze

True story from my own teaching life:

A few years ago, during a photography class, I was explaining aperture and depth of field. I could *see* that at least five students didn't get it. But no one said anything.

Finally, one brave soul raised her hand and asked, "Wait… is depth of field the same as focus?"

I explained it simply- and half the class sighed in relief because they had the same doubt.

Here's the thing: the 'fear of looking dumb' didn't just keep those other students quiet. It robbed them of clarity. It slowed their growth.

And the funniest part? The person who *did* ask the 'dumb' question walked out smarter than everyone else.

The Fear is Universal

Even the greats have it.

- In 1962, a NASA engineer almost didn't ask about a tiny calculation error in a spacecraft trajectory- because he thought might be wrong. That question ended up preventing a crash.
- Davind Bowie once admitted in an interview that early in his career, he prevented to understand music theory jargon just to fit in. He learned much slower because he was afraid to admit ignorance.

The world doesn't remember them for 'looking dumb.' They remember them for what they *did* once they asked.

The Two-Minutes Shame Rule

Here's my philosophy:

If asking a question makes you look dumb for 2 minutes, but not asking it makes you stay dumb for 2 years… always take the 2 minutes.

Pop Culture Proof

- In *Spider-Man: Homecoming*, Peter Parker asks Tony Stark "Why can't I just be like you?" Sounds insecure, right? But that question leads to Stark's mentorship, which changes his whole arc.
- In *Good Will Hunting*, Sean (Robin Williams) calls Will out for pretending to know things he's never experienced. The vulnerability opens the door to real growth.

The Psychology Behind It

Psychologists call this the 'Spotlight Effect'- the belief that people are watching and judging you way more than they actually are.

Truth: most people are too busy thinking about themselves to remember what you asked.

Closer to Home

A student of mine, Amrik, once asked during a review, “Sir, how do you know if your work is actually good or you’re just attached to it?”

It was such an honest, unfiltered question that it sparked a 30-minute discussion that benefited everyone in the room.

The best part? Other students told me later, “I’ve always wondered that, but never dared to ask”

And it took me off to write a book on the beauty of detachment.

Mini Challenge:

Next time you hesitate to ask something, run it through this filter:

- Will knowing the answer help me?
- Am I staying silent because I’m protecting my ego?
- In 5 years, will I regret now knowing this?

If two answers are ‘yes’, ask it. No hesitation.

Chapter 7

Curiosity in Boring Places

(a.k.a. How to Find Fire in the Greyest Rooms)

People think curiosity only lives in exciting, colourful, Instagram-worthy spaces.

Wrong!

Some of the best ideas I've seen were born in fluorescent-lit, windowless classrooms, train stations during power cuts, and government offices that looked like time had stopped in 1978.

The truth? If you can't be curious in a boring place, you're probably not curious at all. You're just riding the high of external stimulation.

The Waiting Room Test

Here’s a simple way to measure your curiosity muscle:

Imagine you’re stuck in a waiting room with nothing but a stack of outdated magazines, a creaky ceiling fan, and an elderly man snoring next to you.

A “meh” mind will just scroll Instar gram until the battery dies.

A curious mind will start wondering:

- Who’s the man sleeping?
- Why is this fan making that rhythm?
- What’s the weirdest story hidden in these old magazines?
- Why does this place smell like a mix of ink and turmeric?

I’ve had some of my best short film ideas come from moments exactly like this.

The Train Station Experiment

Once, I was stuck for 2 hours at Karjat railway station because of a delayed train. Nothing ‘inspiring’ ion sight. Just tea and snacks stalls, vada pav vendors, stray dogs, and luggage carts.

Instead of zoning out, I pulled out my camera and started photographing the patterns: the way steam curled off cutting chai, the yellow paint peeling off a bench, the way two strangers mirrored each other's body language.

By the time the train arrived, I had the seed for a photo series called 'Stillness in Transit', which later got exhibited.

The Science of It

Boredom triggers a search for novelty. The brain starts scanning the environment for anything new or unexpected. That's curiosity trying to save you from mental flatline.

Problem is, most people kill that spark instantly with a distraction (phone, snack, or daydreaming about a holiday).

The trick? Resist the urge to escape. Let boredom push you into micro-discoveries.

Pop Culture Proof

- In *The Office* (US), Jim's funniest pranks on Dwight come from the fact that he's bored at work and that boredom fuels his creativity.
- Sherlock Holmes solves half his cases not because crime scenes are thrilling, but because he notices tiny, boring details nobody else cares about.

Mini Challenge: they Grey Room Game

For the next week, do this:

1. Go somewhere you find painfully boring (waiting room, traffic signal, school corridor).
2. Observe for 5 minutes without your phone.
3. Write down or sketch 3 things you notice that you've never noticed before.

It's going to feel awkward at first. Like your brain is scraping from crumbs- but soon, you'll see patterns and stories everywhere.

Chapter 8

When Curiosity Turns into Noise

(a.k.a. Why Too Many Tabs Open Will Kill Your Brain)

Curiosity is amazing- until it's not.

Think of your mind as a web browser. If you have one or two tabs open, you're focused. If you have 45 tabs open, you're lost, the fan is screaming, and you can't remember where the music is coming from.

That's what happens when curiosity runs wild without direction: everything feels important, but nothing gets done.

The 'YouTube at 2am' Spiral

I once started looking up "how to fix a squeaky tripod" on YouTube. Four hours later, I knew how to make medieval bread, the history of Icelandic horses, and why whales sleep vertically- but my tripod was still squeaky.

Curiosity had hijacked my attention and turned into distraction disguised as learning.

The Case of the Overloaded Student

One of my design students, let's call her Priya, came to me with 17 project ideas for her final year. She was researching all of them at the same time.

Each week she'd show me progress… which was 17 open Google Docs, all half-written.

When she finally killed 14 ideas and focused on 3, she finished a photo-book that got picked up by a small indie publisher.

Moral: Curiosity without editing = mental hoarding.

Science Says…

Our brains have something called **attentional residue-** when you switch tasks too often, a part of your brain stays stuck on the last thing you were doing.

Too many curiosity trails mean you mind becomes a noisy marketplace- voices shouting from every direction, instead of a quiet workshop where you can build something.

Pop Culture Proof

- Tony Stark (*Iron Man*) is a genius inventor because he channels his curiosity into specific problems. If he chased every tech idea he thought of, he'd still be stuck in a garage making robotic coffee mugs.

- Marie Curie didn't win two Nobel Prizes because she explored every branch of science; she went deep into radioactivity and stayed there for decades.

The Filter Rule

When you feel curiosity pulling you in 10 directions:

1. **Ask**: "If I only had 3 months to live, which one would I still want to explore?"
2. **Park the rest** in a 'Later List'- a document, notebook, or even a WhatsApp note to yourself.
3. Give yourself permission to forget them for now.

Mini Challenge: Curiosity Diet

For 7 days:

- Pick one topic you're curious about.
- Ban yourself from deep diving into anything else unless it directly helps this topic.
- Watch how much deeper your insights go.

Chapter 9

Curiosity and Risk

(a.k.a. Why the Best Ideas Feel a Bit Dangerous)

Curiosity is like a compass- it points you somewhere new.

Risk is like a cliff- it asks, “Are you really going to jump?”

The truth: the places curiosity points to are often *outside* your comfort zone. And that’s where the magic is.

The Photographer Who Walked into Danger

Back in 1990, in the boiling heat of South Africa’s township violence, photojournalist Greg Marinovich (yes, my mentor at Harvard) found himself in the middle of a scene most people would sprint away from. Two rival factions were clashing in Soweto. Then- sudden chaos. A man, staggered through the street, engulfed in fire, chased by another wielding a machete.

Every instinct said: get out!

But Greg didn't. He ran closer, lifted his camera, and shot-frame after frame, while trying to make sense of a horror that looked like hell itself unfolding under the afternoon sun.

That single photograph, of a man aflame and another in pursuit, was brutal, searing, unforgettable. It didn't just document violence, it forced the world to stare at a raw truth of apartheid's twilight years.

Risk: Serious injuries/Life-Threatening.

Reward: The Pulitzer Prize

Closer to Home

It happened in 2012. I remember standing on the second-floor lobby of a residential building, in the middle of that restless crowd, watching hundreds of hands rise into the air- different skin tones, all reaching upward, on the way to connect. I knew in that instant: this was *the shot.*

But from that height, it wasn't enough. I needed height, perspective. I turned to my assistant for the wide lens-only to realise he'd vanished for a smoke break. My heart sank for a second, then instinct took over.

I bolted. Two floors up in what felt like seconds, I found myself on the rooftop of a crumbling building. There was no time to think. I leaned out. My pulse was racing, but I clicked. Frame after frame.

That photograph, later titled, 'Hands of Unity', because the most defining image of my career. It won 72 awards across the world. World's most famous photograph tag. National Geographic, United Nations, UNESCO, Smithsonian, HuffPost, Amazon, etc.

The Risk: A slip, a fall?

The Reward: A photograph that still speaks louder than words.

Why Risk and Curiosity Are Siblings

- Curiosity says: "What's over there?"
- Risk says: "You've never been there. It might not be safc."
- Growth happens when you let them both talk… but curiosity get the final word.

The Apollo 11 moon landing? Curiosity about the unknown.

The risk? Possibly not making it back alive.

The result? "One small step for man…" that changed history.

The Comfortable Trap

Most people kill their curiosity at the first sign of discomfort.

"I'd love to try stand-up comedy… but what if I bomb?"

"I want to design my own clothes… but what if no one buys them?"

The irony? The things that scare you a little are often the exact things that can redefine your life.

A Scientific Side Note

Neuroscience shows that risk triggers the same dopamine pathways as reward- meaning your brain literally lights up at the *possibility* of something great happening. That's why we remember risky leaps more than safe steps.

Pop Culture Proof

- *Stanger Things* wouldn't exist if the Duffer Brothers didn't pitch a weird mix of 80s nostalgia, supernatural horror, and kids on bicycles. Studios thought it was 'too odd'. Now it's a global phenomenon.
- Virat Kohli didn't become one of cricket's most dominant players by avoiding aggressive shots- he takes calculated risks every time he bats.

The 15-Second Rule

Next time curiosity pushes you toward something that scares you:

- Give yourself **15 seconds** to say yes before doubt creeps in.
- Send the email. Make the call. Walk into the room.
- You can figure out the 'how' later. Momentum matters more than a perfect plan.

Mini Challenge: Risk Radar

This week, write down:

1. One thing you're curious about that feels slightly risky.
2. The worst that could happen.
3. The best that could happen.

If the best excites you more than the worst scares you- Go for it!

Chapter 10

The Quiet Side of Curiosity

(a.k.a. Why You Sometimes Find Gold

When You're Not Digging)

Curiosity doesn't always roar. Sometimes it whispers.

We tend to imagine curiosity as a restless explorer; constantly hunting, asking, probing. But there's another side to it: the quiet, patient version that watches, waits, and lets the answer come to you.

The Photographer Who Stopped Shooting

There's a Japanese photographer, Rinko Kawauchi, whose work is known for its stillness. She once said she often spends hours just sitting in a place, not taking pictures, until the scene reveals itself.

One afternoon, she sat by a roadside, sipping tea. A shaft of sunlight hit a puddle just right, creating a perfect reflection of cherry blossoms above. She took one frame. That image became one of her most celebrated works.

Sometimes the best shot happens *after* you stop trying to get it.

The Science of Slow Curiosity

Our brains have something called the default mode network; it lights up when we're not focused on a task.

That's why you suddenly get brilliant ideas in the shower, on a walk, or while staring out of a train window.

When you stop digging, your brain starts connecting dots on its own.

Pop Culture Proof

- **J. K. Rowling** thought *Harry Potter* while stuck on a delayed train. She wasn't looking for a book idea. The idea came to her because her mind was idle.
- **Steve Jobs** called this "connecting the dots looking backward"; the connections often appear in quiet reflection, not while aggressively chasing them.

The Indian Tea Stall Lesson

In Kolkata, I once met an old chai seller who had been at the same street corner for 35 years. I asked him why he never expanded or moved. He smiled and said, "If I keep still, everyone passes by here eventually." Curiosity works like that; sometimes you just need to hold ground and let the world reveal itself.

How to Practice Quiet Curiosity

1. **Scheduled Idleness:** Take 20 minutes a day to do nothing. No phone. No notebook. No Laptop. Just sit and watch.
2. **Micro-Observation:** Pick one small thing (like how light falls on your desk) and observe it for 5 minutes.
3. **Delay the Answer:** When faced with a question, resist Googling immediately. Let your mind wrestle with it first.

Mini Challenge: The Non-Search Search

This week, instead of hunting for ideas, create space for them to find you.

- Go for a walk without headphones.
- Sit in a café without opening your laptop.
- Watch a sunset without photographing it.

You might find your next big idea quietly tapping you on the shoulder.

Chapter 11

The Messy Middle

(a.k.a. Where Motivation Goes to Die… and Be Reborn)

Starting something is thrilling.

Finishing something is satisfying.

But the bit in between?

That's the Messy Middle- a swamp of doubt, confusion, and coffee that tastes like regret.

The Half-Built Bridge Problem

Imagine you're building a bridge.

The first few days are exciting- foundations go in, everyone's clapping, pictures are taken. Then comes the endless, repetitive work: bolt after bolt, day after day. You're too far from the start to feel the buzz, too far from the finish to see the payoff.

This is where most projects die.

A Real-World Example: Pixar's Pain Zone

Pixar calls it the *ugly baby phase*. Every new film idea starts as a clumsy, awkward 'baby'- it can't walk, it makes no sense, and honestly, nobody likes it yet.

Andrew Stanton (*Finding Nemo, WALL-E*) once said that midway through every film, the team collectively thinks,

"We should juts start over. This isn't working."

But they don't. They wrestle it into shape, draft after draft, scene after scene. The Magic?

When the finished film hits theatres, no one sees the 3 years of chaos; they only see the final masterpiece.

Closer to Home: The Indian Start-Up Grind

Many Indian start-ups fizzle not because the idea was bad, but because the founders hit the Messy Middle- months of uncertainty with no growth.

Ola, for instance, spent years stuck in "Will this even work?" territory before it became a household name. They pivoted, tweaked, and fought boredom as much as competition.

Why the Middle Hurts So Much

1. **The novelty is gone.**

   The dopamine of 'starting' has worn off.

2. **The reward is too far away.**

   Our brains like short-term wins, and the middle offers almost none.

3. **Uncertainty spikes.**
   You start asking: *Am I wasting my time? Should I quit?*

How to Survive the Messy Middle

- **Shrink the Horizon:** Stop thinking about the finish line. Focus on the next 24 hours.
- **Make the Wins Visible:** Put a sticky note every time you complete something. A wall full of small victories is surprisingly motivating.
- **Get External Energy:** Find people who'll remind you why you started. Sometimes your own enthusiasm won't be enough.

A Story from the Field

When I was producing a student documentary that later went on to win dozens of awards, the middle phase was brutal.

We had reshoots and endless edits, corrupted hard drive, incompatible software, rendering errors, long nights, uncertain days, and some on the verge of quitting.

Looking back, that was the phase that shaped the film.

The choices we made in those stuck, frustrating weeks gave it its soul.

Mini Challenge: The Middle-Only Mindset

If you're stuck in a middle right now:

- Acknowledge it's normal.
- Accept that it's not supported to feel good.
- Keep moving- even one small step is enough.

The Messy Middle isn't a sign you're failing.

It's a sign you're making something worth finishing.

Chapter 12

Accidental Genius

(and Why You're Already Sitting on It)

Some of the greatest breakthroughs in human history weren't the result of perfect planning.

They were… accidents. Happy accidents. Frustrating accidents. Even "Oh no, we broke it" accidents.

The Mistake That Fed the World

In 1928, Alexander Fleming left his petri dishes unattended and went on holiday. When he came back, mold had contaminated his bacterial cultures, ruining his work.

Except… the mold had killed the bacteria.

That mold became penicillin.

That 'ruined experiment' went on to save over 200 million lives.

The Design Flop That Became Fashion

In Japan, denim makers in the 1960s faced a big problem; their jeans were fading unevenly in the wash. It was considered a defect.

But young people loved it.

That 'mistake' gave us the global phenomenon of distressed denim.

The Godfather

Sometimes genius doesn't arrive with a plan; it just walks in, uninvited, like a stray cat. Literally.

The opening of *The Godfather*; that iconic moment where Marlon Brando strokes a cat while quietly deciding people's fates; wasn't scripted. A random cat was just wandering around the Paramount lot that morning, and Coppola, instead of shooing it away, plopped it into Brando's lap, moments before rolling the camera. Boom. Magic. The car kept purring so loudly it actually ruined Brando's audio, and they had to fix it later. But here's the thing: what looked like a technical headache turned into one of the most unforgettable character introductions in cinema. Without planning it, the scene became layered with meaning; soft hands petting, deadly words spoken. Comfort and menace in the same frame.

That's accidental genius: when chaos shows up and instead of shutting the door, you let it in.

Why Accidents Work

1. **They bypass your perfectionism.**

   You stop chasing 'flawless' and start chasing 'what's possible'.

2. They force resourcefulness.
   A glitch demands an immediate, creative fix.
3. They reveal what you didn't know you wanted.
   Some accidents are just prototypes for your best work.

The Real Secret: You Can't Plan Accidents, But You Can Invite Them

- **Experiment More:** The more you try, the more 'mistakes' you'll make.
- **Document Everything:** Keep scraps, drafts, rejected shots. Some will surprise you later.
- **Say Yes Before You're Ready:** You'll learn faster and make more unexpected discoveries.

Closing the Loop

Let’s talk about the unscripted earth- this unpredictable, chaotic, breathtaking planet that doesn’t care about your carefully made plans.

The truth is:

Your work, your career, your creative journey will never go exactly the way you think it will. There will be dead ends, detours, disasters.

And hidden inside those disasters?

Accidental genius.

One Last Thought

You might feel you need to ‘get it right’ before you start.

But every person who made something remarkable began in the same place you are now- uncertain, imperfect, and standing on the edge of the unknown.

You don’t have to know the whole path.

You just have to take the next step…

… and stay curious enough to notice when the wrong turn is actually the right one.

Final Challenge for You

For the next 7 days:

- Try one thing a day you expect to fail at.
- Keep a record of every weird, unplanned result.
- At the end of the week, review them.

You might just find your own penicillin, your own distressed denim.

Because genius doesn't just live in the plan.

It hides in the mess.

About the Author

I've never been good at sitting still. I'm a photographer, filmmaker, professor, and sometimes, by accident, an author. For me, curiosity isn't a fancy word; it's how I survive. It's pushed me onto rooftops, edge of a cliff, or even sleep over a barbed wire when the shot mattered more than safety, into classrooms where students ask the best kind of uncomfortable questions, and into film festivals I never thought I'd see my name in.

When I'm not holding a camera or running a class, I'm usually falling down rabbit holes. Music by Ben Böhmer and Monolink has soundtracked some of my best ideas, leaving me with questions I can't shake off.

And boredom- yes! The restless, irritating kind; has been my most honest collaborator. A lot of my people-winning ideas were born not in moments of inspiration, but in the quiet unease of nothingness.

As a professor, I don't believe my job is to create more artists. My job is to create more human beings who can see the invisible. If education only teaches what is already known, it kills the very curiosity that creates the unknown.

I don't really teach photography, film, or storytelling. I teach how to see. And that changes everything.

These days, I experiment at ITM Skills University's Institute of Design and Media. And teaching is my code language for learning in disguise. Most of my ideas start with the same shrug: IDK.

If you don't spot me in a classroom or on a shoot, I'm probably on a rooftop, or scribbling in an airport notebook, or staring at something ordinary until it becomes extraordinary.

www.ingramcontent.com/pod-product-compliance
Ingram Content Group UK Ltd.
Pitfield, Milton Keynes, MK11 3LW, UK
UKHW040038200726
13845UKWH00054B/470

9 788199 192324